A
Smell
of
Burning
Starts
the
Day

Also by Susan Tichy
The Hands in Exile

Susan Tichy

A
Smell
of
Burning
Starts
the
Day

Wesleyan University Press
Middletown, Connecticut

Acknowledgment is made to the editors of the following journals and an-
thologies, who first published some of these poems: *The American Voice*;
Beloit Poetry Journal; *California Quarterly*; *Crossing the River: Poets of
the Western U.S.* (The Permanent Press, 1987); *Faces and Tongues: Poetry
and Prose about People and War* (Laughing Waters Press, 1986); and
Northwest Review.

I also wish to thank the Eugene M. Kayden Endowment at the University
of Colorado; Jane Berlin and Elinor Nauen, whose financial support was
indispensable; and Kathleen O'Hanlon, without whose assistance I would
never have seen the Philippines. I am additionally indebted to Suzanne
White and Marc Weber, for support and criticism; and to Jeff and Kathy
Babb, Mitchell Kaufman, Lisa Schwartz-Kaufman, Malcolm Richards,
and Todd Jaspers, who made their electricity so generously available.

This book is supported by a grant from the National Endowment for the
Arts.

All inquiries and permissions requests should be addressed to the Pub-
lisher, Wesleyan University Press, 110 Mt. Vernon Street, Middletown,
Connecticut 06457

LIBRARY OF CONGRESS CATALOGING-IN-PUBLICATION DATA
Tichy, Susan, 1952–
  A smell of burning starts the day/Susan Tichy.
    p. cm.
  ISBN 0–8195–2153–1   ISBN 0–8195–1154–4 (pbk.)
  I. Title.
PS3570.I26S6   1988
811'.54—dc19   87–27243
                    CIP

Manufactured in the United States of America

First edition

For Michael,
who went first

Contents

Here
Tarlac Province, Philippines 1985

The lowland is flanked on the west by the jagged Zambales range and on the [north] by the Central Cordillera. Only a few isolated peaks jut out of this plain. The highest of these is . . . Mt. Arayat whose conic symmetry is [made] all the more striking [by] the alluvial flatness of the . . . farmlands for miles around. For many years, that mountain . . . was the physical symbol of . . . defiance. . . . But [dissidents] no longer use Arayat as their base. They have, since the late fifties, intermingled with the life of the plain.

—EDUARDO LACHICA

Capas

"You made a mistake" are the first words
we hear when our feet touch ground.
And they bang the side of the bus
for us, to stop it. "Quickly,
get back on!" Jeepney drivers, children,
women from the market stalls
behind us, even the uniformed man
with a pistol and leather shoes—
crying, "Sir, Ma'am, someone
has fooled you, please, there is nothing
here." It's hotter here than the city,
that's what we notice first, and the lack
of color. But we look east
and it's there—Arayat, a pale blue cone
above the bare exhaustion of the plain.
Bundles of firewood, sacks of charcoal, leaking
a black powder into the dust;
piles of palm hats, bunches of broom-grass,
some still carrying seed; and multicolored
bouquets of plastic shoes—
this we pass in half a block, the crowd trailing
yet hanging back, making no offers
to carry, sell, or direct.
And that's what we notice next,
the caution. Two drivers
come to their senses first: wherever
we mean to be, someone might be paid
to take us. So, when we drag our luggage
into the first open store,
sit down and order beer,
they sit down too, to watch us,
until the one who's braver,
or speaks better English,
or is more in need of money,
asks us where we're from.

Colorado—no, they don't know it.
Rocky Mountains—no, they don't know it.
John Denver—yes, they know him! So,
we are from John Denver, and why are we here?
Are we Air Force, Navy, Marines?
Civilian—but that is a word the woman
who owns the store must translate. And yes,
there are in this half of the province
two hotels. "I will take you,"
says the less bashful driver,
and moves a few feet closer.
But when we begin to negotiate
the price of a day's hire,
based on the price of gas and beer,
our best guess of how much more
than what they need they'll ask for,
we have again this problem—"Ma'am,
there is nothing here. Perhaps
you will let me drive you to the seashore."
So we give the whole list of places
we've come to sea. They're all within
twenty miles of the store we're sitting in, but
we must say it again,
and a third time. At last they begin
to laugh and poke each other,
to talk back and forth so fast
that the only word we recognize
is *revolución*. Yes, we can start with a list
of barangays. Yes we can see them
all in a day—no, two—three at most.
And the mountains, yes, and the bombing range.
"But please do not be disappointed.
There is no scenery, only
like you see here, but worse."
By now the man with sunglasses
is sitting at our table,

and he cannot seem to stop smiling
with his many gold teeth. He has no idea
just what he has gotten into,
but we have accepted his price.
It means he will have a new roof
before the rains begin.
It means he will have a day off
before the end of the year.
It is something like the sky opening,
saying *there will be rice,*
something like the lucky break
his wife has long believed in.
And he wants to start right now,
right away, does not even want
to drink the beer we paid for. He takes
our luggage, seats us, in solitary splendor,
in the twenty-passenger jeep—
and we're off, three innocents, a little
breathless, a little drunk. We leave
pavement, turn left down a line of trees
so the mountain is behind us.
And we're all smiling, all polite, watching
each other in the rear-view mirror.
We've come to see the only thing they have.
He understands. But none of us knows yet
if we can see it, if any word
we have in common names it. We name ourselves
as we speed west, a cloud of dust already
attached to us like a sail.
Anxious to please, he begins to explain
a few things we will need to know.
How his province is poor. How the people farm.
And how in the hills beyond the cane
a few who don't farm live
by hunting orchids, the flowers that grow
on nothing.

At a P.C. Sergeant's House
Zambales Mountains

The food is good: beef, flat fish,
and dog, with vegetables—some of them
parts of trees—and fruit.
We sit under a tree whose branches shade
five hundred square feet of ground,
while the man who brought us tries to explain
who we are. We don't understand,
but they're laughing, just as
on the way here we were told
He is one of the most notorious, like a joke.
In the clearing that makes a barangay,
the jungle is not forgotten, neither
its presence, nor the colors
of its quickly receding face—
on open fires, the white
of rice in blackened pots;
and beside the green of palm leaves, cut
and laid over plates of food,
the red polka-dot dress
of the sergeant's wife. Above that,
her bashful but uncontrollable smile.
Her husband sits with his back to the house,
facing the ragged line
where jungle and the irrigated vines
of squash and eggplant meet.
He wears no uniform, just
a tee-shirt, white on the bulk of his skin.
And you have to admire how clean he looks
on this day of dry-season dust.
You have to admire the calm
with which he displays
no weapons, not even a knife.
"I'll tell you how much they hate him,"
said our friend as we entered the house.

"His wife can cook, but we will be
his only guests for fiesta."
And it's true. There's only us,
and behind the wide trunk of the tree
an old woman crouching
by a blue plastic tub. She washes our dishes
with her head tipped slightly back,
eyes closed, listening
to birds beyond the clearing,
cicadas overhead, and the bell-like laughter
of her two dead sons. The sergeant
never looks at her. His wife
taps one temple, to explain. We nod,
though we will never know
the sacred names of her sons, or
which side they were on. Our friend asks
with his eyes if we understand:
this is not the beginning
of policy; this is the end.
The sergeant eats. The woman
wears nothing under her thin dress
but the dry folds of her skin.
Who we are—he doesn't care.
His smile is vague. His eyes
look for something on the cleared ground
behind us. He ignores us
all—as a hunted animal listens
only for one sound.
We drop the name of his colonel
into the pool of talk
and it lands heavy, it lies there
like a murder weapon no one dares
retrieve though it's in plain sight.

Looking for a Death March Marker

It's called *Primitive Agriculture*
in a photograph of 1899—
the animal, plow, and hut.
Just one of many sidelights to a war.

The animal, plow, and hut
stand at a junction of two roads.
Beyond, a *Typical House*
and family, staring.

In miles of rolling, dry-grass country, all roads lead
to nothing—concrete pylons, legs of towers
they took down and carried away.
At one, a man spreads rice
to dry on a sun-warm slab.

His father was once put off this land:
the towers went up, Saigon went down.
He looks at the air above our heads,
then at the dust-hazed hills.
Beyond them, what? The country
where his son survived the last American war.

Some say a man whose life is saved
owes much. Others,
that we answer to God for what we preserve.
The farmer stirs and separates
the grains with a wooden rake,

and will not say in the miles of grass
which concrete stump is the one.
His eyes move with familiar touch
on acres of dead, burned each year
so the new growth comes in strong.

He shows with his hands how rice
is pressed into balls, wrapped in leaves,
then thrown to a passing prisoner—a skill
that does not change with the shape of the enemy's eyes.

At a Place of Ambush

There is no map
that's accurate. The one on paper
has wrong angles, too few roads,
and names the people living here
don't use. The one in our heads
has too much of one color: red.
It's a color we don't see much of
in the dust-drenched trees. In trees
beyond the sugar cane, a bird repeats
like blades in slow revolution—
clock, clock—
as air the choppers must have cut
like flesh hangs still. . . .
We drive slowly, wave back to boys
on top of a load of hay.
It's the time for drying rice. Women
pause from work, to watch us weave
through squares of grain in the road.
A few protect the crop from birds
with old sacks, sewn together
in a heavy net. The rest use children,
naked, or almost naked, armed
with sticks. And pigs must be prodded
out of sleep and to their feet—
for ours is the only car. Our jeepney
sports three chrome horses
on the hood, two more on the long roof,
window fringe in four colors,
and several dedications to the saints;
but it's us they stare at, grinning,
or laughing out loud at the very idea—
Americans, here. Lines of huts
with their bare dirt yards,
their laundry and tethered chickens,
wander from high ground to low,

like a sluggish stream
from which a dozing carabao
once blundered to its feet like a god. . . .
Along that river, a child
carried another child,
shielding its eyes from light
glinting around the bodies
turning like slow propellers
dressed in rags. . . .
"What are you looking?" a woman calls.
I can't say, "At what we see." I shout,
"Just looking. To say hello." She laughs
and covers her mouth with her hand.
Maybe because of my answer, maybe because
she has spoken English, and we have understood.
Return everything you borrow. Do not
take a single needle or thread
from the people. . . . Trees at the bridge
grow dense as hair, shielding the tarmac face
from light. Here in the damp,
men went naked, but wrapped in cloth
the metal of their guns. . . . Small boys run
beside the car, pounding the fenders, trying
to touch our dangling arms.
Their feet and legs are pale with dust,
their shouts loud, their fingers sharp.
We are sixty miles from Manila,
three from the smooth North Road.
And how beautiful are the red flowers
blooming in rusted Crisco cans
on the steps of the poorest houses.

from Liquidation Is a Metaphor

I did not know his name
was the same as mine.
He was riding in a tricycle.
We followed in our car.
He stopped near the grounds
of an elementary school
where I walked up to him
in the presence of several children.
I shot him in the head.
It was only later I learned
that when my relatives heard the news
they went there to claim my body.
That is why I remember this
one incident so well.

Photograph, Agta Bowman

They wave us out
of the jeep—buy
plants, buy brightly
painted arrows,
too small to kill.
When I actually come
the women fade, the boy
stops laughing, the man
uncoils from the ground,
stands with his bow
that kills,
his young goat sleeping,
tethered, at his feet.
In his hand a dozen
bamboo arrows, tips filed
from metal gleaned
on the U.S. bombing range—
these points for birds,
these for small game—
their flat shapes traditional
as grass
which binds them to the shaft.
The man doesn't smile,
but holds the gaze of the camera.
Around him, orchids.
Around him, a bright
white light,
which on film he seems
to have taken into himself.
Nothing else.
But his family is here,
visible in the skill
with which his bow
is strung.
In their silence, I am here.
And history is here;
it's a tool.

Here

It is sometimes from dawn
till well after dark, shaking the poles
of the houses, shaking a person's
feet, and shaking the orchids.

American Air Force.
Philippine Air Force.
American Navy
from carriers out on the bay.
They think the sierra is nothing,
think there is no obstacle
between them and the explosion.

And there isn't.
Those dark figures are men
bent double by the weight of livelihood.

We have lived this way for a long time.

And the others, who come here to use the noise,
to accustom themselves to the trembling—
by the world's largest bombing range,
the world's largest rebel target-practice camp—

Are they your people?

We ourselves are our only people.
We farm, we weave, we gather orchids
and sell them. We gather steel.

And they don't come anymore. Not many
people come here anymore.

No planes today, and no wind. But something
moves in the water
so a shiver goes through the rice.
It's beautiful here. It's here

they stopped the landlord
in broad daylight with his son
and cut them into pieces with their knives.

In Fact

At the river a woman washing her face
hangs a pink towel over her head:
a kind of wall. In our group

we have nothing to do—
the cliffs blue and red, the light
wide open and white. We're guests

and lucky enough to be women: you men
can have your hour of talk. Down here
they stare when I roll up my pants

at the size of my calves, the white.
I don't know when their silence means
they're bashful, or when I've done

a wrong thing. This is
the first time I've been wholly female,
the first time we've been apart.

The river is wide, shallow, and slow.
There are places for laundry,
places for talk. I wade with children

who show me places where bodies
have sometimes been found in the rocks.
Are there fish? Not many. They've all

been eaten, along with the dogs and birds.
The water is cool, the stones
a slippery shade of mauve.

If I close my eyes I see
just one of the unexplainables—
that half-built house we passed this morning

where a man anxious to marry
takes time to weave dark patterns
in the walls.

Barangay Fiesta: A Captain

for my husband

He wears a striped, civilian shirt
over new fatigue pants, tennis shoes.
I saw him enter the village, shed boots
and camouflage shirt. We were coming up
from the river, a gaggle of women:
he never looked. His men are now
spread out in the trees and houses.
He holds his beer like any man,
and he holds an arc of stillness
in the faces and bodies of other men.
Their chairs ring the latticed yard
of the barangay leader's house,
and their silence squats, a familiar guest,
in the bare dirt center.
It is permitted, now, to speak,
so the barangay leader is saying,
"Nineteen years are enough." He says it
without expression, and everyone stares
at nothing, as if he has said it might rain.
You are just as bad. When the captain asks,
"What is your mission here?" you shrug.

It's the same when the singers come—
two guitars, and the girl has a voice much larger
than the thin cotton dress she wears.
It is permitted, now, to sing
"The Ballad of Ninoy Aquino," so
she does—*The soldiers were there*;
for some reason they could do nothing.
But if she could sing without breathing
I think she would. She never quite looks
at the first circle—the captain, you, a dozen
important, immobile men. Around you,
your women and children, free to mingle
with the bare feet and shining rifles

of Civilian Home Defense. Around us,
a bamboo fence. Then the rest of the town
like a chorus staring in at the central cast.

—A hundred people. Their faces range
from the old bow-maker, brown
and thin, to a woman whose cheeks are swollen
and pale as her nursing tit. From a stick
in the hand of her fat child,
a plastic helicopter
dangles upside down, brushing the arm
of a young man who bangs the fence
out of time to the strummed guitar.
He seems drunk, but isn't. That look
of inward concentration is a scar.

And it stays quiet. Though no one
looks directly at this captain,
they know when he leans an elbow
on one knee, accepts a cigarette,
or turns his head. "I'm afraid,"
says the barangay leader, smiling faintly
at you, "our holidays here are few."

—"But happy," says the captain.
When he pays for the music, no one smiles.
Even the baby is still, watching the plastic gunship
fish air behind the heads
of three seated, solemn men.
Two girls in love with the same boy
giggle in the crisscross shade. But not one person
claps hands, taps a foot, or sways—
although it is permitted, now, to dance.

The Bus from Sagada:
Passing a Sacred Mountain

The man is trying to talk the boy
into giving me a flower. The boy
has been eating his flowers,
petal by petal, rolling each one
between his palms, then peeling away
the long yellow fibers, placing
the sweet pink between his lips.
Now he puts his shoes on the seat in front
and grins his small embarrassment.
I am large and single, like a calla.
He is just one of the Everlasting.
But the man is still prodding his shoulder—
he won't stop. So the boy,
though he's only seven or eight,
sits up straight with his hands on his knees:
there is something he has to do.

This flower has been carried from the boy's home.
Perhaps it was given to him. Perhaps he pulled it
from a neighbor's bush as he passed.
It's damp, when he hands it to me, and cool.
One petal has been torn away
and a drop of nectar dangles at the wound.
The man is talking a mile a minute,
and laughing. The boy is shy.
And I don't know if I'm expected
to eat the flower too.
I decide not. Steam

is beginning to rise from the carrots
and cauliflower packed in over the engine.
The night guard, on his way back to town,
sits dozing over his rifle. He too is damp,

and just a boy, with red wool socks
pulled over the legs of his trousers.
"*Pulag*," says the man with the grin, and points
to one dark side
of the mountain I had forgotten.

Galang

Manila, where the single open eye
of a child looked back at me
from a torn basket
on pavement.

Without anger there is no hope,
so taught the great
uncle of all who hope.

In his country now the angry slay
the angry. Ports are closed.

*

Turning a corner into a street
of flowers. Behind the flowers, children
play with a sick cat, push it
into a puddle, into a pile
of flowers burning.

In their lives, no walls.

*

So you follow the teachings.
You have this treasure, compassion,
and you spread it among the poor.
Soon you get scared, like a rich man.
When it's gone, what will you do?

*

Go on. Stop
at a table made from cardboard,
covered in cloth.
You smoke, so buy one
of these three cigarettes for sale.

Buy another. Light it
for the boy who counts your change.

Keep going. Step into the path
of a cop. Say you're sorry
as fruit rolls under your knees, and the one
he's chasing turns the corner.

 *

I know the diamond is wrapped in this cloth,
so wrote the great lover
of God and wine.

A drunk shouts,
"Why are you laughing?"
and follows down the street.

"He has not always been one of us,"
they tell me.
First he was a teacher,
Next he was a prisoner.
Now he is a teacher
of fools.

 *

In the mountains, a beggar
keeps his eyes cast down,
his cup raised, his body
crouched in its smallest shape,

and does not touch the stone
wall of the bank behind him.

For the poor are always with us,
so taught the great speaker
of riddles.

 *

At a place between towns, a woman
washes herself at a pump.
She wears a bra, and washes
over, under, around it, guards
the arbitrary privacy
of two handfuls of flesh.

It is everything.

*

How simple to say life is simple
where the sucking mouth gets its share of dust.
The barrio women seem hardly to know
they are climbed on, tugged at, scratched
by all these children, precious
and parasitic as orchids.

*

Just walking around I learn—
wood is scarce, water pumped
by foot. And only two things
are done here: talk and work.
I can't do either. I sit.

And a man on a carabao, looking at me,
lets it carry him into a grove of trees.

*

An island.
Sand floats in the whiskey,
lies on my tongue
long after the ebb of talk.

—The goodness of food.
—The economics of exploitation.
—The history of revolt.

"Please, Ma'am, eat more."

"My number-one boyfriend
comes back next week
from Detroit."

"The army kills our carabao.
They eat, but we cannot plow."

Two tourists,
four boatmen,
and a whore.

*

But I saw the revolution, once.
It looked like a tired man
who said, "My house is yours,"

I said, "No, mine is yours."

We kept that up—
mine, yours,
mine, yours,
mine, yours.

*

At a creek, three men are washing
—two peasants
and a builder of tunnels.

The countryside surrounds the city.
It is what he came to teach them,
yet he feels surprise

when the one he calls
No-Write-No-Read
picks up a gun to kill him.

     *

Go on, but slow:
the gait

of a carabao holds the jeep
in a cloud of its own dust.

Black hair white,
white skin brown.

If you're trapped
it is not by this. The fist

that bangs the side of the open jeep
is small. A child of six—

she points to me, giggles,
and salutes.

The Arrest of Dante: Our Chains

"Believe me, son. The most loving man on earth cannot justify the pain he causes the most undeserving wife during the supreme moment of childbirth. You men!" Her spittle sounded like a coin striking flat against the mud.

Walking there in the dark and unmindful of the rain, he said to himself: If it be true that I can never be worthy of the love of my wife, well then, I will justify myself to my child.
—STEVAN JAVELLANA

When my wife was near her time
I imagined many things, even dreamed
a wet black monkey
was biting her melon breasts.
She doesn't have melon breasts.
She's thin, like me, her cheeks
two shiny walnuts under my thumbs.
We had to work hard to make a child
the few times we were together.
Good work, like planting
rice in a field of blood. We used to laugh
that the army would take the child,
study its face to find
in the wrinkled, mysterious skin
my likeness. I don't know why we laughed.
They would have speared our baby
as soon as a cat they were bored with. . . .
One night, I woke wet
in the cool mountains, fire
eating me into something hard
and lasting, like a native boat.
Death's always here, perched deep
in the branches of my lungs.
But this was more. I feared
she would give me up,
take the child to be raised
under one roof, under the lie. . . .
To be free of the land
was my first dream, but there I was,

walking where pebbles were scattered
and ruts were deep, past sleeping stores
and Coca-Cola signs,
in a hurry because I imagined
they were dressing my child in the wrong clothes—
gray and many and buttoned high up to its chin.
I thought of the hands that made such clothing—
too many hands. I thought of the white
European hands I envied, the first to pen
You have nothing to lose. . . .
I passed the walled-in house
of my *compadre*. He's rich
and has the vices of the rich—
obesity, and the willingness to use.
A cock was already crowing
when I passed the house of my brother,
just one among the squatter shacks
steadied by the long wall
of the Goodyear Service Center.
His vices are the vices of the poor—
too quick a hand, and patience.
Then the *municipo,* standing
on the spot where we burned it down. . . .
I went unarmed. I had dreamed
of a child born in my likeness
with a gun instead of a heart,
dreamed of men, intent and drab,
who circled for generations
the moment of feathers and blood.
Don't come, she told me.
*Stay away, think of me
when you pierce some other woman.*
So I knew, even
as my big hands made their furrows
in her hair, she blamed me every time
steel severed a peasant's neck

and the rest danced mad as chickens.
Death rides on me
like flies on the eyes of a great strong carabao bull. . . .
In my second dream the land rose
like heaven above the towns.
I built a house where a child
could be both honest and strong—
my child. —Or is it?
How many nights did I lie with her?
How many nights was she left
to talk with whomever she pleased?
Oh, and she pleased many—white teeth, eyes
opaque as polished wood.
She's strong, but a willing man
can dig deep in her flesh. . . .
Those nights in the tunnels—
in my mind a light, in my body
that river of boiling blood—
there were no women. I saved myself
for my enemies. And they knew me not—
the man with a sack, the man on a bike,
less visible than their fears.
Why should I stay away?
I'm him—the merchant of death,
mechanic of dreams, sailor on
the sea of resistance that drowns them.
What would she bear? A child
pure as hatred, or a monkey
black as the heart? Whatever it was, it would reap
the fragile grain of remembrance.
It would stand on the neck of at least one
of the owners of the dead. . . .
I closed my teeth and kept going,
not even thinking it odd
that a group of men should gather
at a not yet open store.

They nodded as I passed, my throat full
like a basket woven so tight
not a drop of water escapes.
I would be too late
for the agony. . . . There
was the house she lived in.
A light still burned
at one small shaded window.
I walked faster. And there
was my grandfather's hand on my shoulder,
his voice that I used to hear
when just before the rain a wind
went silvery through the rice.
He said, *The land is a good wife.*
And then they knew me.

"Mabuhay NPA"

Those who trust us educate us.
　　—GEORGE ELIOT

In your house are four pieces of furniture—
couch, chair, cabinet,
and a table where two can sit.
We sit, and your shy wife
sets rice, *tinapá,* vinegar, salt
before us. Her sister has gone to a barrio store,
so there is, for my husband, beer,
and, for me, a Coke and a glass
with a piece of ice.
You are standing, talking
of the day you built this house. Sun dazzles
through palm walls, and I'm thinking

of what my husband told me about water.
Deadly is the word he used. When he lived here
half the children died. And I've seen,
in three days, two funerals, the coffin
not straining the arms of the four men
who carried it down the road. But it was
a long time ago he lived here
and since then much has changed.
The children still leave school
at ten. They marry young—
it is all you have, each other—
and die old at any age. You're speaking

of your mother's death, your father's wife,
of the church and how you choose
—*Católic* or *Iglesia*—not
by faith, but by the hours of the mass.
For you work on the day of rest.
But some things change.
In twenty years the government
has paved roads and drilled wells
and killed. You can drive now in two hours

31

from the slums of Manila, penned behind muraled walls
and false house fronts, palms growing
on the filled-in bay. What can't be penned

is people. Moved out one hundred thousand
at a time, they come back, put up a shack so small
the children sleep in the daytime
while their parents work the streets,
selling cigarettes one at a time; streets
where a child of nine who sells herself
for a dollar or two is proud
to have risen above her family.
All night with a foreign man—it is
the first bed she has ever seen. . . .
Here, too, the worst is hidden. You know
how to move aside, how to hide what hurts

behind an eye that watches though it never looks.
Five years of peace in this province.
Five years of cockfights, business.
You can walk down the street, as you could not then,
and see them—the brother
of a man found in a shot-up jeep; the major
who ordered death over dinner; a boy
who was six when he found his first body
face-down by the Bamban Bridge.
Less visible are the women, some
who were raped, one whose baby
was drop-kicked into a wall. The roads

go to every barangay. So does the telephone,
so do the armed informants called
Civilian Home Defense, and the heavily
guarded workers who dig the wells. . . .
So I think the ice is pure now, when it's dumped
from the freezer into the cart of the man
with three fingers on his right hand.

He pushes the block in front of his knees,
under awnings and soft-drink signs,
baskets and hanging flowers.
In front of each customer's store
he takes his rusted, large-toothed saw

and cuts, carefully drawing sawdust
over the new, clean wound.
What's left at the end of the row of shops
he wheels to the market, leaves
with vegetable scraps and chickens
under the stall of a woman
who sells garlic, ginger, and peas.
She too has a saw, and when ice is wanted
it's dragged out into the open, cut,
and dragged back, forming a pool that runs with others
under the hands of egg-washers, pans of rotting fish.
With his pay, the old man drinks,

and when he sees Americans, he follows them
and calls them, "Brother, where are you going?"
When he was young he stood in this street
throwing balls of rice to prisoners
climbing from the trains. So now,
when he stands before us, shouting
in an old, split voice, his neighbors don't smile
though he's toothless and ugly and strange.
What's real is not for shame. This man
was a chemical engineer. "They beat me.
They beat me and beat me and beat me."
Then "Shhh . . ." He puts his fingers to his lips,
and the stumps are blue and shiny
like the fine blade of a *bolo*.
How he lives on his few pesos
is a matter of family pride. You work
twelve hours a day, seven days a week,
while at night, the highway by your house

is quiet for three hours. "The road is life,"
you say, though it means no rest. As you speak,
a Volkswagen stops outside. They are buying three trays
of fish, these people in shorts and polo shirts.
They could be kings—with those teeth, with that car
like a jewel resting on a blanket of palm and heat.

And you too seem drunk with the story you tell
in clear words—*hatred, hope.*
In your bloodshot eyes there is no distance
between vision and flesh. Though stooped
from working what you will never own,
you straighten when you speak. . . . When we think of the
   future
we think of distance, the thousands
of miles, hours, islands—but here it is, here
in the blood excitement makes visible
under your skin. Even when you remember
yourself, your guests, when you tell us,

"I am sorry. Eat." When you ask, "Forgive me
for speaking of my troubles . . ." All this time
the ice is melting in my glass. All this time
the man who wheels it through the street
is sleeping through the killing heat of one day.
You say, "I think we will count the years
till we see each other again."
But the tears you bring to my eyes
run into the dust on my face; they vanish.
For here is your life—family pictures
on this wall like any other. And you think
when you say "They must let us live"

that you are not speaking of us.
For we too keep a secret well—our fear
that the future will be decided
not in words but in our bodies. . . .

"A good shot," you said this morning
where branches of mango feathered over a wall.
Two words; and I thought as I tried for focus,
for patterns of leaf and sun,
how you could not tell if the author
fell dead ten feet from the wall.
Was she one of those smiling schoolgirls,
whose bright uniforms flutter all over the town,

or younger, one of the children
who sometimes just touch my skin.
For luck, they say. . . .
Could you see from where you were standing
how my hand shook, how I worried
less about the P.C.—that sudden
black they make in daylight—
than about my camera settings?
How would I capture that bright,
clear red, color of revolution
and love . . . ? "You will tell this story,"
you say. And you too think luck has come,

a pair of strangers, who sit at your table,
eat your food. But I'm no fool, I don't want
what lives here, what feeds on you.
Long ago I read that even a man in prison
can be free. And it was easy, I thought,
that clean separation of ourselves. . . .
When a duck walks into the house
you call out, "Hello, Easter dinner!"
then smile when your daughter lays her cheek
on its spotted head. It's still a cage
of ribs—is that the story?
I know it did not help you
that I picked up my glass and drank.

Inheritance: The Water Cure

Provoked by the memory of my great-great-uncle Colonel John W. Bubb, Commander of Tarlac Province, 1899–1902.

We are now living in a heroic age of human history, from the opening of which many of our own people recoil with misgiving, as though we were of choice and de novo *entering upon a questionable enterprise, the remote consequences of which must inevitably prove disastrous to all concerned.*
    —ARTHUR MACARTHUR, *Military Governor of the Philippines, testifying before the U.S. Senate, 1902*

I know you think I'm becoming a nag; but I want to record the whole family, with not one lost.
    —JOHN W. BUBB, *to his brother*

Prelude: 1956

The windows of the house are two, so we
are blind to the east and south.
A fine damp glazes the barrel of my rifle.

I don't feel young. And the others,
three or four men like me,
have cracked like figures on an old canvas.

The weight of things is suddenly great.
Our seventeen bullets. Our wet food.
Beyond those trees is the world.
I think of it as a face I will never see again.

I must have a family,
but I don't think of them.
I must have a language,
but I don't speak. I would say,

"I'm not a man, I'm a child."
But there is nothing now
anxiety can gain.

The moment is long.
Wind pushes up on the floor of the house,
and I think, *Not yet.*
I remember the boots,
palm walls gray with rain.

And our faces shine a little,
though there is no source of light.
A sign that this is not the work of a master.

One

We were proud of him in my family,
called him "The General"
he later became,
though his campaign ribbons meant nothing to us—
Slim Buttes, the Coeur d'Alene, and this:
> *The uncooperative official*
> *was spread-eagled on his back*
> *and the end of a hose*
> *was run into his mouth.*

In Tarlac there were no hoses.
This was the old days—horses,
the cumbersome Krag.
They poured it in
from buckets, salted and cold,
three times, four, a dozen. . . .
To his mother, a man who kneed
the swollen stomachs wrote,
I am in my glory. But in our house

there was no war, only a War
Department—good jobs, right
company, a name. No one cried
at the kitchen table. No one swore
in the living room, or drank.
We never said *nigger, shut up,*
or *no.* We spoke to strangers,
ate from a tablecloth, fed
our animals well. His portrait

was there with the others, his daughter
a treasured guest, the first woman
I knew to live her own life.
Art was a god, Manila
the place she had entertained

with classic blue-willow china
we dared not touch. If we laughed,
it was at her interesting hats,
not books she gave

to children who wanted toys—
the first verse, the first taste
of salt from other shores.
"To circle the world means coming home,"
I wrote of those adventures. The stars
weren't fixed but never strayed, made possible
the great plot, the charted course,
gesture of light, specific
in the darkness of infinity.

They stood above the rituals—
greeting and apology, punishment and play,
the touch of hands spotted with age,
smell of a clean room, where love, like duty,
is measured by the silence that surrounds it.
Silence was a door between the inner
and outer dark, opened by her voice,
the feel of the root of words as it spread
and deepened. . . .

          There's no doubt he never
touched a prisoner. There's no doubt he gave
his orders in perfect speech. I know because
whatever I know of honor I learned
from them—to speak up, to imagine. . . .
I contrived to live outwardly
the life of a little boy.
So wrote the son
of one of the men he tortured.

Two

From the beginning, the general said,
*you must understand that a soldier
has a human heart.* He spends his passion
in pure coin, and what he recalls is the fine play
of dawn on the daily life—voice
of a comrade, voice of a pure soprano singing
an old song of love. . . .

No soldier says, "We let the wounded die."
He says, *There was one I recall
we took to the hospital and treated.* He says

I saw the column of smoke,
but not the fire.

    *

On the plain between Arayat
and the blue western hills
sugar cane is burning
in plumes arced like dancers, anchored
by a thin toe of flame.
They rise between bright acres
of new-transplanted rice—an act
of husbandry, not war,
though through those head-high grasses
a man can move unseen.

But, said the general, called to account,
*these people of whom I speak
do not know what* independence *means.
They think it is something to eat.*

And I hear the call to order,
threat of the rhythm
of grass in wind, those waves

that drown lines of fence that would hold them in.
For the civilized thing is the reticent thing,
the drawn shade, the second thought,
the memory carefully stored
like a fragile plant on cotton. . . .

   * *1900* *

. . . I can see him now, that blue-eyed, friendly man
relaxed under our nipa palms, his gun beside him,
"at the ready" for our fathers in hiding.
And on his knee the brown, sweat-stained cover
of the first English book in Tarlac.
    I see the cat.
    Do you see the cat?
    Does the cat see me?
The boy had a word, *friend,*
to fix on the daily temptation,
the love song sung by soldiers far from home,
and the round, exotic fruit called *apple.*
It was not that he had not seen his neighbor
hanging in the town park. *Luis,* he would say,
and again, *Luis,* turning over
what he remembered—callused heels
a foot above his head, a crust
already forming on the man's last sweat.
It was that there was no one
to whom he could speak of this—
not his mother, who had told him
not to go near the park.
And certainly not those big, pale men
discarding blue wool shirts for khaki, smiling,
and showing their hairy chests.
It was not that he did not know
those muscles had killed men.
It was that they were no more

than big, good-natured boys
whom boredom made patient. So that,
with time, even a child more timid,
less conscious than himself
could see the strange black markings
as a cat. Years later, when he entered school,
he would pick up a pen and write,
My name is Carlos. I am three years old.
Three years old—when he heard his parents whisper,
when the blank thing entered his father's eyes.
It was not that he did not see.
It was that he had already learned
that wise colonial gift—
to trust his enemies, to love them
for the fine line that makes a portrait
out of the rendered face. As a man he wrote,
Friendship had nothing to do with war.
It had no effect on my hatred.
By then he would say he understood
the memory of his father's torture—vivid
because it had a name.

     *

Do you know the nigger slave?
Do you know the parrot's perch?
Do you know the word *falanga,*
or the San Juanico Bridge?
Do you know which make of field telephone
delivers the biggest shock?

In Tarlac, 1985, young men in a barangay smile.
They want to talk, but cover themselves
to the eyes when I touch my camera.
    I see the *insurrecto.*
    Do you see the *insurrecto*?
    Does the *insurrecto* see me?

. . . I see them swollen,
pregnant under the knee
of a man who looks like me.
Then water, *like an artesian well,*
shoots three or four feet in the air.
They say this is a reliable cure
for silence. And when night is torn
by a shout it is sometimes mine.

For I was not given that pure coin
to be thrown in a sewage ditch.
I was not asked to remember
what happened to someone else.
Sweat on my face is the cool
side of a pitcher of water.
Blue-willow china, eighty years old:
the water inside is pink.

"Don't look," says the warning voice of dream—
at the bloody arms of a dead child
thrown over its head in surrender.
Emotions are for private use.
We knew this from the day we learned
to read in the same language.

Three

We blow every nigger to nigger heaven,
wrote one American boy,
though it turned out to be

a joke, whole cloth, just something
to jolly the old folks at home.
What he meant was, *We*

are planting our traditions
in such a way that they never
can be removed from the soil, an act

of husbandry, not war. For though
the interest of other governments
may be judged by the foreign capital

invested in the country, ours is judged
by whether the people *rise to call*
the name of the U.S. blessed. . . .

And they do. You ought to see them—
Spanish- or Asian-looking men
with names like Bobby, Buddy, Chuck. . . .

You would see the natives
coming back from the hills
carrying little white flags

on sticks. And only two
or three times
were all of them shot.

Under orders to take no prisoners,
what else could they do?
. . . She was beautiful,

the one they spared—
the corporal admitted this.
But they set a good example

by taking turns together
in the democratic spirit—officers
and men. . . . Don't blame them. Sent by God

to establish system where chaos reigns,
they did their best, taught English,
from which *the natives might imbibe the spirit*

of Anglo-Saxon ways. Faced, as they were,
by a climate in which the best of men
degenerate as to indolence, yet one

*where every foot of the way
is a revelation of riches,* a place in
a paroxysmal state of excitement, possessed

suddenly by themselves, their own
high spirits and self-confidence, their
absolute ignorance of the Philippine archipelago,

they rose to the opportunity to *hold, govern,
and control.* And though the far-Eastern sun
gave *boundless scope for indulgence*

of the boldest assumptions,
their own blood, blooming in wild profusion,
was *the first they ever heard of independence.* . . .
    Remember,

they knew nothing but what the natives told them.
They had no intelligence
but their own. . . . *What fixes the right*

of a man in the upper class
to demand the services
of a man in the lower class? This was what

they wanted to know, the law they thought
would civilize the country
for whom Christ also died.

And they understood the answer, as men began
to surrender their ancient weapons, as women began
to surrender their ancient wares, as ships began

to unload teachers and surplus American goods—.
They called it *a great uplifting.*
They called it *debt.*

Four

In *traje de tigre* a man faces a camera
on the wall of his dead grandson's house.
He is *tall for a native,* and stands on one leg
with the other cocked, his eyes
filled with a sacred mountain of disdain.
Against him was mounted *the first recorded action
against a known guerrilla.*

Underbrush mauled their leggings, mocked
the two-thousand accurate yards
of a Krag's smokeless bite. The hill
was steep *and annoyed by fire,* the *real*
empty except for the prisoners—two
from Capas, and three cooks who'd wandered,
searching, as always, for chickens. They were found

in a fearful condition, two being dead,
the rest mangled, and no two able
to agree on a single story of whom to blame.
It's certain they had been underfed.
It's certain that certain *playful Filipinos*
triggered empty pistols at their heads.
It's certain Don Mianong was jailed.

"Take care of the child," were his last words,
years after the *spacious innocence*
of the Tarlac frontier had died. A planter, he was,
a man of place; not one of *Los Indios Bravos,*
men of the mind, who named themselves
for extravagant tricks of daring staged
by Buffalo Bill in Paris. . . . *Los indios,*

said the Spanish, were hardly capable
of rebelling; and shipped their leaders,
bound hand and foot, carried like packets

of merchandise, back to Manila,
there to be tortured, or drowned.
And the hapless *Yanqui* made the same mistake.
Los Indios Bravos—a doctor, a chemist,

a painter who once painted cash
on a tablecloth, slipped out the door. . . .
So it was the *Yanqui* could never create
a dependable distinction between town and hill,
could never, even by grace of the hose,
know whom he was talking to, who
might answer. And even before the rain the war

was fluid, with no ground held;
every battle fought would be fought again.
Men *fell as though shot* by the sun,
marched without wagons, which sank to the box
in lakes the maps called roads,
ate what they found, paid with fever,
useless paper, and what they called

an irritable heart. For the enemy's strength,
though it seemed to sink, was a bamboo raft, designed
to float just under the surface. . . .
So, *with a regiment on sick report*
and half the column insane,
they took the *real* a third time,
took Don Mianong's surrender.

"I achieved a rank in prison,"
he liked to tell his sons. "*Capataz de lavanderos*—
laundry foreman . . ." In *traje de tigre*
he stands on the wall of his grandson's house
as overhead swells *a roof like a mountain.*
To the heart's fortress there is no path—
something the *Yanqui* might have learned

before he scaled such difficult heights,
and fell into *the ambush of civilized men*;
that is, created the camp and dead line,
beyond which anything moving is made to die. . . .
Outside, the swamps and *wooded, mist-making hills*
are gone—*under the plowshare,*
under the sword. He was gentle with girls,

as though they were gamecocks, tough
with boys, *as though they were troops*—.
"When the *Yanquis* came,
they found two prisoners dead."
He said it as if who swung the *bolo*
was none of his concern. He said it as if
every battle fought would have to be fought again.

Five: 1876

When I wake from this dream I am always wet,
summer or winter, at home or at sea
en route to other wars. It's pleasure,
at first, lying still in the ebb of fear.
Then the chill sets in. For this,
like all important messages,
is tied to the body. Something we learned
from the savages. Something we taught our men
with patience and the backs of our hands.
I am a courier in this dream,
not Commissary, as I was in fact.
And I bring the news from Crazy Horse,
his word: to make war on all soldiers
who once touch the waters of the Tongue.
Lesser things may ride behind you,
tied to the saddle, tied to a mule, but this
you remember: they burned our grass,
two hundred miles of charred ground, a million flies
taking residence in our eyes. Yet,
hunting was good, and fishing. I first caught
that gentle lunacy there. I was Staff,
exempt from dispensing discipline
to two thousand bored men and mules.
By the guard tent, four stakes
were driven into the ground,
a drunken soldier stretched out and tied. . . .
but not by me. I caught fifty-five trout
in one day, eighty the next.
And we ate them all, washed down
with letters from home—our first
and last. We fancied ourselves
cut off from the feminine world,
which meant to us *civilization.*
So we carried it with us, invented—
like Pyle, who compared the face
of each flower to his bride.

We sketched, we read, we shot rare birds
for the General. We measured their wings,
and at night the stars,
whose positions changed more than our own.
I slept with my letters, hoping to dream
my daughter's laugh, my wife's cross voice,
anything but the songs
our Crow scouts sang to the moon.
They sang for the noise of it, sang to be part
of a quiet so great *a shot fired*
by the man in the moon would be heard
among those mountains. I know now:
they were the quiet's tongue. In the dream,
when I stand with my messages close to my heart,
I'm dressed like an Indian, holding a trout
in my left hand, holding a gun in my right.
I don't know what kind. It is like
the Rosebud, where all the Indians in the world
lined up in front of our guns
and we couldn't tell Sioux from Crow so we killed
no one. We were at full strength then,
the Major still sane, the horses full
of two-day grass, and *wild roses by the thousands*
laying their delicate beauties at our feet. . . .
But though I have come
to the dark banks of the Powder,
I do not speak. I stand there, still
as the bluffs of copper, coal, and gold—
that message all must pass, and read.
I'm spared so much in the dream—the blind march
through smoke and fog; the night march, lit
by a side of burning mountain;
and those brass-eagle buttons, with bones,
we found in a bed of ashes. . . .
I held their message in my mouth
those hours above Dead Canyon,

when our Long Toms were talking
and I thought the Sioux would have me.
Now they do. And the sweat reminds me
that under our clothes we are always naked, dressed
in *the unseen ray of the star of glory*. . . .
At the Yellowstone, *you could stand like a pelican*
letting the rain run off your back. No tents,
not enough food. Just thunder,
to add Satanic grandeur to the scene.
We were paid there—paper, not coin—
and marched south—. But not in the dream.
It's torture to stand there, making signs
to those who pass, with their fifteen days' rations,
issued by me, to march
their fifty-two days toward the center of hell.
For hell isn't fire, it's water. Twenty-six days
of rain, wind, the gumbo balled up
on boots and hooves, with Indians
always before us, their wide trail
like the bed of a ghostly river through the grass.
I was still Commissary. It meant I hid chocolate
and beans for the sickest. Salt and tea
dissolved on muleback, trickled in light
and dark streams down the animals' legs.
On the Little Missouri
we had two antelope, scraps of hardtack,
a half-dozen rosebushes under guard.
But once past the Heart we were past hope too.
We marched like dead men, perfumed
by thousands of trampled flowers. My butcher,
who had never cut up a horse before,
or a man, had much to learn.
No wood for eighty-six miles. We burned sage
or ate the horses raw. I was glad
to be sent ahead, glad to escape
men I loved, who lay where they fell,

contorted, as if bucked and gagged
in the Old Army way. For a man never knows
how much farther he will go.
We found the village that very night:
from two miles away we smelled meat.
And that's where I am, in the dream,
I know it now: there, at the siege
we laid to that miserable ditch. I stand at the edge
of a light like moonlight, a dark like smoke,
and I can't see the source of either.
Like men on canvas, we seem not to hear
the moans of the dying, the calling souls
of the dead. We step over them,
tear captured buffalo meat into pieces. . . .
It was like that. I was there. I saw Big Bat
ingeniously using a captive squaw
to shield himself from the bullets.
I saw him prove that scalping is an art.
And I heard the children, whose crying even
our rain of hell into that dugout couldn't quell.
I was there, and you will read
that *in true forlorn-hope fashion*
I *behaved in a gallant manner.*
It means I fought. And I saw the best of the food
to the mouths of the worst of the men.
I listened to what the captives had to say.
Then I slept. I heard shots, and slept again.
By morning there were fewer captives.
I mounted a horse *with characteristic dash*
and rode. . . . But I never reach Deadwood
in this dream. I stand there,
watching that man ride south
on a captured Indian pony.
He looks the same, but behind him now
rides his eternal family—a squaw's body,
of which there seemed to be no unwounded part,

and the old chief, cradling not a child
but his own guts in his arms. It's what I must do—
watch. As a man watches a surgeon
insert wire, looped at the end,
into the wound along an arrow shaft,
watches as if he were two men. . . .
I don't want to be two men.
I don't want to feel how sweat
runs down an Indian thigh.
I lie in the wet sheets, testing myself,
trying to hear beyond the clock
my daughter's cat crossing the hall. . . .
"You get through
by becoming a man who gets through."
That's what an old scout taught me.
I think of the Major, not raving,
but calmly digging Indians
out of his ear with a fork. . . . For years
I have carried next to my skin
these messages I am not permitted to read.
I bring them forth as an Indian sings
what he hears in the silent air—.
Don't be a fool. Whether with drums
or a sutler's poison whiskey, make prayers
before you touch the waters of the Tongue.

Six

* 1901 *
From a little spot of sogginess
in a *reconcentrado* pen
bats swirled
in orgies
over the smallpox dead—
the suburbs of hell. Hell

was farther south,
province
of a veteran of Wounded
Knee. There, the body
of a priest hung, a censer
over the heads of thirteen

hundred souls,
their last confessions carried
from his face and ears
by flies.
It took them weeks
to dig their own graves,

to climb in and stand
at attention,
in neat squads of twenty,
with riflemen working six days,
and resting
on the last.

* 1970 *
Yet it could be made
entirely civilized
according to the general's

personal theory of war.
Officers take coffee breaks
in air-conditioned Angeles,

get back by noon
to count the bodies
face-down over the dikes.

These numbers are
important, but
so is the gold haze of dust

that makes Arayat a pale breast
under a slip of silk—.
The enemy always

counts the dead, *fanatical
in grief,
fanatical in*

revenge. He does not know
the rules of war
or count the flies

that jewel the lip—
a crust of emerald
over the crust of blood.

* *1981* *
So here, where roads are new,
soldiers are burying heads. Boys,
perhaps, no more than twenty,
or men with a passion for cards.
Work done, they rest in the shade, smoke
from their cigarettes rising

straight up through tattered leaves.
No tax in the export zones.
No strikes in the lumber mills. And
as to the scruples of conscience,
the governor did not
understand what the question implied.

I said soldiers are burying heads.
First, they stuff the mouths—
with genitals, or fruit. Not
to shock the relatives, who may
find the careless grave, but just
to amuse themselves. It's hot

and there is no one
to whom they can tell the secrets
of their hearts.
That is why they have granted
the beauty queen of Palapag
a few spare hours of life.

Said a West Point lieutenant,
The fun was fast and furious
as they scurried down like monkeys
from their long-legged huts.
A child said, *I
played dead beside my mother.*

But though it was, as promised,
like a turkey shoot,
still there is no one
to whom they can tell the secrets of their hearts.
Not the Germans, digging chromite;
not the British, cutting trees;

and not the Japs or Yankees, who forget the past
in the depths of the copper mines. These are
not concerned with internal affairs;
except to note that a soldier,
once home with his work and family,
forfeits the privilege

of a prisoner of war, becomes no more
than *a murderer, a thief,* if he fights because
independence means something to eat. . . .
Now soldiers are resting from burying heads.
They smoke, and rifles lean on their arms
like lovers. To amuse themselves,

they stop a bus on the new road, search
for weapons, as instructed, and
steal cabbages off the roof—
one young one pitching them down
as hard as he can at the old.
A man who notices blood on their uniforms

lays that secret deep
in the many folds of his heart.
For there is no external enemy,
only the native, *cruel to animals,*
only the mind, *recording such conclusions
as its own actions should suggest.* So,

*when you consider the difficulties
of the Commissary Department, the Quartermaster
   Department,*
you see why it's here, where roads are new,
that soldiers are burying heads.
And the beauty queen of Palapag
has visited the chambers of their hearts.

"We're God here," the torturers say,
in the system where chaos reigns.
She was displayed *trussed like a pig*
so her long hair dragged the ground.
Said the senator: speaking of freedom now
is the reading of Job's lamentations

at a wedding feast.

Seven

The Bamban hills are a dark day, carved
and thumbed to resemble rock. *Tarlac,*
beyond, is the Spanish name for a weed. . . .
We know they crossed the river

in a great typhoon. We know there was
a *dissident ecology,* some baleful combination
of history, language, and land

that makes a man believe his freedom
is ordained by God. We know they came
by foot and horse, because the rail was blown.

We don't know that he used buckets.
There were kerosene cans, syringes,
tubes in the nose, or just the throat
held open by a large hand.

And we don't know that he kneeled.
Sometimes they jumped. Or a big man
would strike the pit of the stomach
with his fist. We know each time
the whip fell blood would come.

This could be slander. Maybe he turned
his back with a clenched jaw,
or yelled at a captain
when the memo crossed his desk.
Maybe his hand shook at the memory
of his daughter's beautiful speech. . . .

The child who told on him
was three.
At ten they were considered
old enough to wield a knife—

I want no prisoners.
I want all persons killed
who are capable
of bearing arms against us.

Three years old, when his
anonymous soldier-father
crept home for clothes and food.
Three years old when Baldwin's *Primer*
first taught him *to see . . .*

In competent hands, not one
of the *cures* is lethal—
not the *water,* not the *rope,*

not the journey of partial drowning
whose rings keep spreading, whose visions insist
on telling you who you are.

If the heart doesn't fail . . .
If a line doesn't break
where the fragile map
of the brain is drawn in blood . . .

In our house there were flooded fields,
rice in a bowl of hands
held to a starving face.
And ways to stop fearing this dream.

"To circle the world means coming home,"
I write on a plastic tabletop
in a dusty store in Tarlac.
Outside, stars of lamplight
mark the barrios, lighting rooms
where old hands still
brush hair from the eyes of the young;

stars as far as the river,
where in darkness a pure soprano
begins to sing of love. . . .

On the hot plain around me
the bougainvillaea blooms,
that native bush the Spanish named
and planted near their beds:
its fragrant wind is not enough
to hush the other voices.

Injun, nigger, beggar-man, thief—
that old song
of darkness threatening light.

"Be careful,
be careful when you speak."

In a field the corpse of an old man
was clutching a wounded child.

Notes

The Philippine-American War—known to Americans as the Philippine Insurrection—was fought officially from February 4, 1899, to July 4, 1902. Twenty-four thousand combatants and perhaps a half-million civilians died between those dates. Unofficially, fighting continued in the southern islands for an additional eleven years. At issue was the fate of the Philippines following the short-lived Spanish-American War: the United States had sailed into a flourishing revolution, which it manipulated but refused to recognize. As the Philippine Republic was declared at Malolos, near Manila, the United States signed a treaty with Spain and annexed the islands as its first and only colony.

The ensuing war included only nine months of conventional fighting. In November 1899, the Republic dissolved at Tarlac Town (now Tarlac City), seventy miles north of Manila. As the main American force drove the Filipino general and president, Emilio Aguinaldo, north to the cordillera, Colonel John W. Bubb took command of Tarlac Province. The scattered nationalists returned to the kind of warfare they knew best, and to the leadership of the men they knew best—the local gentry. In Tarlac, their first guerrilla general was Servillano Aquino ("Don Mianong"), grandfather of Benigno "Ninoy" Aquino, Jr.

The Filipinos, untrained and underarmed, had been weak opponents in frontal combat, and the Americans expected to spend 1900 mopping up a war that was over. Instead, in the first year of the century their combat casualties doubled, with all the increase in the number of men killed. In an army already exhausted from campaigning in a tropical climate, terror and frustration soon took their toll in discipline and in the will of line officers to pursue the "benevolent" occupation policies of their superiors.

There had been, from the beginning, elements who were unable or unwilling to distinguish between warfare and slaughter. These were mostly fired-up volunteers, anxious to "get a nigger" and some glory. But the army regulars, being veterans of the Indian campaigns, were no strangers to racism and genocide either. Most of their senior officers—including Bubb—had been fighting all their adult lives, from Bull Run on, and had lived lives of effective isolation from the civilian world. Events of 1900 caused many of these officers to advocate scorched-earth policies—including mass deportation, imprisonment, and execution—as suitable treatment for natives who were, in the words of Bubb's superior, General Lloyd Wheaton, "without a redeeming feature of character." Though the most extreme measures recommended by Wheaton and his sympathizers never became policy, it became increasingly a matter of an officer's personal disposition whether they were applied within his command. In Camiling, Tarlac, one witness to the water torture and execution of civilians was Carlos Romulo, Jr., a precocious three-year-old who would one day be aide-de-camp to Douglas MacArthur and the first president of the United Nations General Assembly.

Eventually, the American strategy of "harsh pacification" combined with propaganda and civil-affairs programs had the desired effect, and today it is cited as a model for counter-guerrilla campaigns. Those historians who stress the benefits of popular education and other inducements to the Filipino populace generally forget that the now-familiar techniques of hamleting and free-fire zones ("dead lines") were perfected in this war, and that thousands died of smallpox and death sentence in huge *reconcentrados,* whose earlier use by the Spanish in Cuba had been cited as proof of the humanitarian motives of the *Yanqui* as he launched the war that led him to the archipelago. In all, the ratio of Filipino killed to wounded was 5:1, exactly the opposite of the contemporary Boer War.

For their part, the Filipino *insurrectos* perfected a system of double or shadow government, in which apparently *amigo* officials of towns and barrios were controlled by or identical to the local *insurrecto* leadership—a system that still flourishes today.

Since the 1930s, Filipino dissidence has increasingly assumed a communist vocabulary and ideology. The New People's Army, current avatar of this unbroken tradition, was founded in Capas, Tarlac, in 1969. By 1986, more soldiers were at war in the Philippines than the U.S. fielded at the height of its conquest, and Filipino peasants held less land than they did when the Spanish fell.

P. 4. A *barangay* is a village or a district of a larger town. Used interchangeably with *barrio.*

P. 6. The *P.C.* is the Philippine Constabulary.

P.8. Survivors of the Bataan *Death March* were interned at Capas. A U.S. Navy radio station stands on the site today.

P. 11. A *carabao* is a water buffalo.

P. 12. A *tricycle* is a motorbike with a sidecar, used as a taxi. The poem *"from* Liquidation Is a Metaphor" is distilled from an affidavit executed for the Subcommittee on Asian and Pacific Affairs of the Foreign Affairs Committee of the U.S. House of Representatives by a former intelligence operative of the Philippine Constabulary in Tarlac Province.

P. 13. The *Agtas,* called Negritos, are an aboriginal people occupying marginal land throughout the archipelago.

P. 22. *Galang,* literally "grace," is the custom of respecting the dignity of others. From the Pampango, a Philippine language.

P. 27. Bernabé Buscayno, *"Commander Dante,"* a tubercular peasant from Capas, was founder of the New People's Army of the Philippines in 1969.

P. 31. *Mabuhay* is a greeting translatable as "welcome" or "long-live." *Tinapá* is a kind of smoked fish. The *Iglesia ni Cristo* is a Christian sect native to the Philippines. A *boli* is a long-bladed knife, comparable to a machete.

P. 37. Italicized portions of "Inheritance: The Water Cure" are from numerous sources among them: Carlos Romulo, Jr.'s *I Walked with Heroes,* Nick Joaquin's *The Aquinos of Tarlac,* Joseph Schott's *The Ordeal of Samar,* William Sexton's *Soldiers in the Sun*; standard sources n the 1876 Sioux campaign, including John Burke's *On the Border with Crook,* John Finerty's *War-Path and Bivouac*; testimony given before the U.S. Senate Committee on the Philippines in 1902 testimony given before nongovernmental hearing following a massacre of civilians on Samar in 1981; American newspaper accounts of 1899 to 1902; orders and dispatches issued by U.S. officers in the Philippines; and the diaries and letters of U.S. servicemen.

I prefer to leave the enlisted men anonymous; it is enough to say that one served under Colonel Bubb. Others quoted include William Howard Taft, first Civil Governor of the Philippines, later President of the United States; Admiral George Dewey; Generals Arthur MacArthur, Robert P. Hughes, and Jacob Smith; and Senators Edward W. Carmack, Joseph L. Rawlins, Albert Jeremiah Beveridge, and Henry Cabot Lodge.

The *Krag-Jorgensen* and the *Long Tom* (a modified Springfield) were rifles used by the U.S. infantry. *The nigger slave* (from the Syrian: *al-'abd al-Aswad*) is an electrical apparatus for inserting a heated skewer into the anus. *The parrot's perch* (Chilean: *pau de arara*) is a horizontal pole from which a victim is suspended by the knees, head downward, with wrists bound to the ankles. *Falanga* (or *falaka*; Turkish, but now widespread) means beating the soles of the feet. *The San Juanico Bridge* was named for the suspension bridge linking Imelda Marcos's home island, Leyte, to Samar—a birthday present from her husband. It requires the victim to lie with the head on one table and feet on another, holding the body level in between. The *rope cure,* used by Americans in the Philippines, involved tying the head and torso together with a rope behind the back, then twisting the rope with a stick, a procedure that resulted in confession, strangulation, or a broken neck.

Big Bat Pourrier was a white army scout. The battle described in "Five: 1876" took place in October at Slim Buttes, Dakota Territory, between units of the 5th Cavalry and a band of Sioux led by one of the two chiefs known to whites as American Horse. The cavalry was escorting Bubb in an attempt to reach Deadwood and obtain food for the starving men of General Crook's column. The engagement was the last of a summer campaign which began in April and included more than 2,000 miles of marching for infantry and horse.

ABOUT THE AUTHOR

Susan Tichy began this book in Tarlac, Central Luzon, where she had gone with her husband to do research for a novel. While working on the first poems she learned of her own legacy, a great-uncle who was part of the occupying army at the turn of the century and in brutal command of Tarlac itself. She lives in Rosita, a ghost town near Westcliffe, Colorado, where she works as a free-lance writer of poems, articles, and, under a pseudonym, genre fiction. She is resident artist for the Colorado Council on the Arts and Humanities. In fall 1988 she will move to Virginia to teach English at George Mason University.

Tichy received her B.A. from Goddard College in 1975 and her M.A. from the University of Colorado in 1979. Her first book, *The Hands in Exile,* was a 1983 selection of the National Poetry Series and in 1985 won the Eugene Kayden Award for Poetry of the University of Colorado. Her poem "At a P.C. Sergeant's House" won a 1987–88 Pushcart Prize.

ABOUT THE BOOK

A Smell of Burning Starts the Day was composed on Mergenthaler Linotron 202 in Sabon. Sabon was designed by the late Swiss typographer, teacher, scholar, book designer, and type designer Jan Tschichold.

The book was composed by Brevis Press in Bethany, Connecticut, and designed by Kachergis Book Design of Pittsboro, North Carolina.

Wesleyan University Press, 1988.